CELTIC
RENAISSANCE

CELTIC RENAISSANCE

A Coloring Book by Alice Rigan

HARPER COLOPHON BOOKS
Harper & Row, Publishers
New York, Cambridge, Philadelphia, San Francisco
London, Mexico City, São Paulo, Sydney

acknowledgements

It is quite impossible to thank adequately and by name all
those who played a part in the evolution of this book. However,
I do especially wish to thank: my husband, Terry Ryan, for
his continual support; John Button and Stephen Clark for
their patience in answering my numerous questions concern-
ing the making of a book; Susan Miller-Collins, for her assist-
ance in the transcription of several of the designs; Stan Stan-
field for his typing and proofing skills; Sir George Trevelyan
for his enthusiastic encouragement; and all of the good people
at Findhorn Publications for their support and the joy they
bring to my working day.

This work was first published jointly in Scotland by Findhorn Publications and The Thule Press.

First HARPER COLOPHON edition published 1982.

ISBN: 0-06-090946-3 (previously ISBN: 0-906191-43-3)

82 83 84 85 10 9 8 7 6 5 4 3 2 1

by Sir George Trevelyan

FOREWORD

A REVIVAL of Celtic art as an aspect of the spiritual awakening in our times is surely to be welcomed. This renaissance is not a dry academic study of a long vanished culture, but a recognition that the Celtic folk-soul was in ancient days a channel for the eternal and ageless wisdom.

We are again discovering the essential concept of the vast oneness of being which is the ground of all existence. We know again that our earth is a living organism within the greater organism of the universe, ultimately spiritual in its nature. We are recovering the knowledge of the etheric world, that vast structure of vital energies through which the realm of divine archetypal ideas is poured into the visible forms of nature.

Our normal senses cannot today comprehend the etheric, and must therefore rely on research into the material world. With the development of acute self-consciousness and intellect in the last three centuries, we have lost the capacity to 'see' the etheric world and with it the realm of the nature spirits, the kingdom of the Great God Pan. The reason for this loss is simply that the organs of subtler perception have atrophied within us all as the price we have to pay for the development of our very 'masculine' intellects. It does not mean that elemental and angelic beings do not exist or are mere superstition. Our forebearers still possessed these faculties of more 'feminine' perception into the oneness of life within all form.

It is one of the major functions of art to make visible the invisible. Does this not give us a fresh clue to the amazing complexity of the interweaving and flowing forms of Celtic art? Is this not an attempt to express the vision of the etheric life creatively at work with the whole of nature? Look at that splendid book *Sensitive Chaos* by Schwenk, in which with brilliant photography he shows the parallels between the vortices of flowing water and the shapes in plant forms, growing trees, geological formations and the ever-changing clouds. So ephemeral are these patterns in water that the eye alone cannot capture them, but the inner eye can set them down for us in art. Look at such masterpieces at *The Book of Kells* in this light and a new meaning comes to the symbols.

Our age of spiritual awakening is the age of rediscovering the etheric world, and it is not surprising that it also heralds a revival of Celtic art and symbolism, for it is through the symbolism of the arts — including myth and fairy story — that the deeper truths are spoken. A symbol is open to interpretation on many levels, and if it speaks to us on a deeper level and enhances the meaning of life for us, who can say that our interpretation is untrue simply because there are other interpretations?

So look again at Celtic art as a gateway to the etheric, and at Alice Rigan's achievement in these designs. Let the eye roam through these extraordinary forms until it begins to perceive the flow of life through apparently still matter and our inner vision awakens the sleeping princess.

Alice has shown us how these ancient forms, deeply studied and mastered, can be used to express new age thoughts. The connection is valid, and her work will help us to bring alive in ourselves the Celtic stream of inner wisdom. Ours is an age of breakthrough into esoteric knowledge. Art must play its part in touching the soul through beauty of form, and help the inner eye of the mind to see and reanimate the life of Alice's brilliant designs. To work into them in the way she suggests is truly a process of heightening consciousness.

INTRODUCTION

RARELY DOES SOMETHING come from nothing. I can remember a game we played as children called cat's cradle. One player would arrange a continuous loop of string in a pattern that flowed from the fingers of one hand to the fingers of the other. Then the entire arrangement would be transferred to the hands of the next player, who added an extra twist to the string, thus creating a new design. The game continued as long as each player in turn could create a new form from the old.

The evolution of art throughout history parallels the game of cat's cradle, with the peak of any art style being the collective effort of generations of artists. The ancient culture and peoples that we know as Celtic are an excellent example, for the Celtic artists were people who adapted traditional forms to new uses, and used creatively the art of the cultures that surrounded them. The masterpieces which they so ingeniously created are unique, and might therefore be thought by some to be totally new, yet Celtic art is in fact a synthesis of many pre-existing art forms, skilfully adapted to match changing needs.

Similarly, my drawings are not totally new, yet they are not copies of the old. They are an attempt to breathe new life into a spirit that has lain dormant for centuries, original designs with a new twist to the traditional style of Celtic art. With their zeal for new forms and creative alternatives, the Celtic artists would have been quick to affirm that the inability to change is death in art, and the power to adapt is life.

Within weeks of my arrival in Scotland in 1977, I began to see signs that a slumbering giant was stirring and about to reawaken. Over the last few decades, interest in Celtic art as it was during its peak of sacred expression has gradually increased. Having landed in the heart of northern Scotland with little knowledge of its social or artistic history, and certainly with no plans to become actively involved in it, I soon found myself with pencil in hand trying to create something which might resemble the remnants of the Celtic art that I saw all around me. Perhaps my naïveté was to my advantage, for with no prior knowledge of Scottish history I was not influenced by preconceptions in thought or technique. All I was aware of was a fascination for the style and a desire to communicate my own thoughts.

A flurry of encouraging comments and compliments edged me onward, and simultaneously fanned my curiosity as to why so many people were touched in some way by these seemingly simple line drawings, especially since my creations had no historical value, being my own creations and not copies of the old. I live in a community that receives large numbers of guests from all parts of the world, and those who expressed the most interest could not be neatly categorised. Coming from many nations and professions as they did, I could not justify their interest as purely historical, pride in their own heritage, or because they were students of art. It was not until months later, when I went to live on the small west coast island of Erraid, that I began to understand the potential magic of this art and why it had flourished in years past.

Erraid possesses an earthy ruggedness, the landscape composed of jagged rocks and only such foliage as is low enough to be spared by the ocean winds. There is little on the island to distract one from the basic elements of living. From the front door of our granite cottage you could see the island of Mull and all of the eastern coastline of Iona. It was on Iona, and other islands like it off the coasts of northern Britain, that the Celtic monks lived, worked, worshipped and created their sacred manuscripts. Here, surrounded by the ocean and the elements, I became aware of life's rhythms.

Rhythm surrounds us and embraces our every movement; it is the centre of every living thing. Steadily we breathe, exchanging essential ingredients with our environment. With each change in the tide the earth is breathing as well, her massive chest swelling and contracting twice daily. The moon cycle, the seasons, life and death, our pulse, the migration of birds — all share a characteristic steady rhythm. I began to see a predictable pattern in things; a life rhythm, the cycles varying from fractions of a second to millenia. It is the one element that is rooted so deeply in each of us that its presence has become

purely instinctive. Rarely are we consciously aware of it and of the security that we derive from it; yet should our heart skip a beat, should the moon fail to rise or the tide not come in, should spring move to autumn and miss out summer entirely, we would immediately notice that something odd had happened.

It is no wonder that the early peoples of our world, so attuned to the nature of the earth and the skies, always seemed to have a pattern that dances through their art, a thread that twists and shapes itself in a pattern filled with rhythm. The line may be thick or thin, angular, curvilinear, decisive or meandering. It may be totally predictable, or move about in lyrical dances that bring sparks of humour to the more serious message. Whatever its character, the line moves through and around; becomes a part of the other elements in the drawing. It becomes the life force that binds all the other parts of the story being told in the design. Since a primary aim of the manuscript artist was to communicate a sacred message, this rhythmic line is undoubtedly one of the most effective ways of symbolising the divine life force that links and unites all things together.

Perhaps, then, those people who find themselves attracted to Celtic art are reacting to their own basic instincts, and whether consciously or not are reacting to a symbol of life and unity. The patterns, suggesting the quiet and beautiful rhythms of nature, are a soothing influence on

those who are now choosing to de-emphasise the effect of the mechanised age and return more to their natural element. Obviously, the next turn in the evolutionary spiral of Celtic art has arrived.

Some time ago I became aware of the mounting frustrations of a young artistic friend. He was deeply disappointed that no one seemed to understand the message he sought to communicate through his paintings. In working with him through the problems of symbolism and its interpretation, I began to comprehend the importance of one's choice of symbols. If the goal of artists through their paintings, poets through their poems, or singers through their songs is to express and fulfil only themselves, then how they paint, write or sing is a purely personal matter. But if the goal is to communicate feelings or messages to others, then the perceptions of the audience must be considered. To expect to be understood by a person who speaks only Japanese, a knowledge of French is useless. In the same way, if one's aim as an artist is to communicate a concept or story, and the audience does not understand the symbolism, then a common language must be found that can link the artist's creative imagination with that of the audience.

Times change, and many early symbols are not now fully understood. We have been brought up in a culture that perceives our environment and ourselves very differently from our distant ancestors. Our awareness and use of symbols in our everyday activities and our meditations and religious ceremonies is less than ever before, and they have largely become a mysterious language of the past. Since my aim is to communicate basic concepts of spiritual evolution and planetary unity, I must choose symbols with modern and widespread recognition. We all understand and relate to the language of the human body because we all possess one. Subconsciously, too, we all respond to the symbolism contained in rhythm. Therefore, the Celtic technique of decoration using knots and spirals, coupled with a design centred on a human form that conveys a concept or story, is the ideal medium for my message.

How or where to begin with a drawing that will end up as a delicately choreographed dance can be baffling unless the message of the design has been established first. Without this central theme it is easy to become tangled in knots and interlacing patterns, and overwhelmed by the mounting complexity of the design. In this respect I can thank the very nature of Celtic art for being my teacher, for its complexity alone would make it virtually impossible to create a design if I became more involved with the detail than with the message. If the central theme is kept in mind at all times, the lavish ornamentation emerges organically from the theme to embrace and enhance it.

I worked with a pencil and rubber eraser. The full design would not be apparent in the early stages, but the message, often derived from a dream or meditation, would be. A preliminary sketch enabled me to determine the basic format, into which an arrangement of figures could be placed to express the central theme. Once they seemed to be in the appropriate places, the remainder of the drawing was simply to emphasise and decorate the figures and their environment.

Once started, most of the drawings took between one and three days to complete. As long as the message was uppermost in my mind, the drawing unfolded with speed; if the ornamentation took the upper hand, I inevitably encountered obstacles. When the drawing was going well I became absorbed in it for hours at a stretch, and began to experience something of what art historians might be suggesting when they say that the work of the Celtic monks was a result of meditation and communion with God.

Drawing these designs has become a meditation. When involved in the rhythm of the lines, the peacefulness and harmony that the lines symbolise and invoke seem to embrace me. The faces of the people are generally untouched from the first attempt, and I have grown to marvel at the variety of personalities that emerges if I move quickly and loosely with the pencil. To think too deeply about how a face or body position should appear inevitably results in an awkward or overworked image. If one person ends up playing with another's toes, or leaning on her friend's shoulder, it only becomes apparent after they have already taken up their positions and assumed their natural postures.

Often I sit with a design for hours after its completion, and feel as though I am seeing it for the first time. I acknowledge that it was my hand and pencil that drew it, yet I wonder why I feel no personal attachment to the drawings. I am simply grateful to them for what they are teaching me.

I have seen the designs grow from thoughts in meditation to drawings on paper, and work their way out into the world through stationery, greeting cards, jewellery and book illustrations. The response from people from around the world at first overwhelmed me, until I began to realise the magnitude of the universal subsonscious desire to revive and renew this ancient art form.

I have stumbled accidentally into a game of cat's cradle, for the designs you now see have taken a new twist from Celtic drawings done many centuries ago. Through the medium of this book, I invite you to join in the renaissance of Celtic art by becoming personally involved. I pass the string over to you, the next player, to add yet another twist.

HISTORY

THE CELTS appeared on the historical scene in the early Bronze Age. At this time — the latter part of the fifth century B.C. — they were primarily a central European culture; but they soon stretched from Spain to Scandinavia and from Galatia in Asia Minor to the Atlantic coasts of Britain and Ireland. The Celts had no empire, for they had no central government. They were a mass of independent tribes or clans, free to act separately when they so chose, or to form confederacies for common action if necessity demanded. Communication between them was difficult and slow; yet in language, myth, ritual, belief, literature and art, they were one.

They were brave and warlike people, using horses and chariots, and had already made considerable advances in agriculture. They were acquainted with the use of iron and other metals, and with the arts of weaving and dyeing. Their skill in metalwork and weaving can be gathered from the following passage from the Roman writer Diadorus Siculus, of the first century B.C.: "They wear bracelets and armlets, and around their necks thick rings, all of gold, and costly finger rings, and even golden corselets: they have dyed tunics, flowered with colours of every kind, and striped cloaks fastened with a brooch, and divided into numerous many-coloured squares."

Yet, skilled as they were in the arts and crafts, these Celts of the pre-Christian period lacked a written language. Their history and traditions were handed down by word of mouth from generation to generation by an order of bards — highly trained poets whose duty was to learn, recite and compose poems dealing with these matters. Religion was taught and justice administered by the Druids, who taught "to worship God, to do nothing evil, and to practice bravery."

During the first century B.C., the Celts of the continent, who had come into contact with Greece and Rome through war or trade, learned to use the Greek alphabet. It was only after the introduction of Christianity to the surviving Celtic nations of the west that the Roman alphabet was adopted and modified to commit Celtic speech to writing.

To understand and appreciate fully the art of these pre-Christian-era Celts, it is necessary to understand the distinction between two fundamentally different styles of artistic expression. One is what is called representative or naturalistic art — art which attempts to represent or to imitate what is seen in nature. The other is abstract or geometric art. It imitates nothing; it constructs ornamental designs by means of a pleasing combination of flowing lines and decorative patterns. It is full of fancy and imagination, and depends in a special way on a keen sense of rhythm, balance and proportion. If occasionally some of its motifs appear to be suggestive of naturalistic forms, such as waves or leaves, or bird or animal heads, these are never attempts at direct portrayal, but are strongly stylised, and introduced merely as parts of a decorative geometric scheme. This was the natural medium through which the Celts found their artistic expression.

So great was their genius for geometric art that by developing originally simple themes, and gradually incorporating the artistic influences of foreign cultures into them, they evolved a peculiar and distinctive style that would later have a profound effect on the art of the emerging Western culture.

As the Celts spread out over the continent, their trade and contact with other nations expanded, exposing them to many styles and techniques of art. However, they were no mere copyists of their neighbours. They readily borrowed foreign ideas and developed them according to their own taste, producing themes and styles that expressed clearly their Celtic individuality. For example, their artistic impulse de-emphasised purely aesthetic objects such as statues or architectural monuments. Instead, they created objects that were of daily use, and then beautified these with decorative curvilinear designs. Their armour and the harnesses of their horses, their tools and personal ornaments, were things which they valued highly and therefore found worthy of being decorated by the best artistic skill possible.

The objects produced by Celtic craftsmen were of elegant form and pleasing proportions. Decoration was always appropriate, applied with restraint and not over-loaded. One element which maintains its presence throughout the history of Celtic art is the quality of rhythmic movement evoked by the flowing contours and graceful curves of the lines. There is a lyrical and spontaneous quality, which paved the way for the later introduction of humour into the designs. Above all, Celtic art is alive and vibrant; it is never boring.

During this entire pre-Christian era the Celtic art styles have been termed La Téne I (500-300 B.C.), La Téne II (300-100 B.C.), and La Téne III (100 B.C. to the Christian Era). Generally speaking, these phases mark the development, peak, and then gradual decline of Celtic art style on the continent.

During La Téne II and III, Rome extended her conquests over all the Celtic lands of the continent, and by the beginning of the Christian Era, the Celts of Asia Minor, Spain, Italy, Gaul and the Danube region were all subject to Roman power. Through their final and complete subjugation to the Romans, the Celts lost more than their liberty; they lost also that natural individuality and independence of thought which had expressed itself in a distinctive style of art. The imagination and idealism which is the very nature of artistic genius seems to blossom only when nations control their own destiny; so it is no wonder that the rapid extinction of the art of the continental Celts coincides with the Roman rise.

During these last few centuries B.C., bands of Celtic immigrants were steadily crossing over to the British Isles and colonising them. These colonists

brought with them not only objects of art produced on the continent, but also the craftsmen who could produce them. Here the La Téne style continued to flourish into the Christian Era, years beyond its decline on the continent.

Gradually the Roman involvement in southern Britain increased until, in 43 A.D., the Roman government became the primary power. As on the continent, the gradual loss of freedom experienced by the Celts was again followed by a decline in their unique art style, becoming most obvious by the second century A.D. But the British Celts never became as thoroughly Romanised as those on the continent, so their artistry was never completely lost. The Celts' native artistic genius in fact reasserted itself, and began to embellish and give character to certain of the imported Roman art forms; but in so doing lost much of its individual character.

Further north, where Roman influence was less, the Celts were free enough to maintain their artistic traditions. Ireland did not see much of the Romans, and in Scotland the legions intermittently occupied only the central part of the lowlands for about four generations from 80 to 211 A.D. Hence the northern school of Celtic design continued to develop, reasonably undisturbed, during this period.

During the latter part of the Roman period, from 250 to 410 A.D., Celtic art in Britain went through a dark period. Generally, the little that was produced is considered weak and diluted in style, and has been called 'the Ultimate La Téne', a name which appears to brand these efforts as the last expiring flicker of the old La Téne tradition.

In 410 A.D. the Romans retreated from Britain. Following the Romans, the British Celts faced another couple of centuries of disturbances from the Saxons, invaders coming from western Europe. Remarkably, in spite of wars, disorders and subjugations, there were still a few Celtic craftsmen left, capable of giving rise to another revival. And it is this revival that had great influence on the eventual artistic achievements of Ireland and Scotland.

Britain was an island experiencing a continuous influx of new peoples. The Celts were only one of many such waves, moving from east to west across the island. They adjoined and greatly influenced the Britons who arrived before them, and in turn were strongly affected by the waves of new peoples who followed. It is no wonder that much of the strongest surviving proof of Celtic art, in spite of its origins throughout the European continent, is to be found in the westernmost parts of Europe, Scotland, and Ireland. In these areas — Ireland and the greater part of Scotland — the Celtic populace remained largely undisturbed. They carried the old traditions in their art, and were seen to achieve their greatest masterpieces in the form of illuminated manuscripts. Here, in the quiet and seclusion of the Irish Christian monasteries, the Celtic artist-craftsman could continue to evolve his decorative schemes of flowing lines and graceful curves by beautifying the pages of the Gospels, each copy of which had to be laboriously copied out by hand, word for word.

The elaborate decorations which adorn the borders of the pages often become a part of a word, or a letter, or in some cases embrace an entire page. Rich in imagination and profoundly impressive in their detail and complexity, these decorations serve to fulfil two purposes: communication and illumination. Communication, because the stories told by the symbolism within the decoration related the essence of the message of the written word. With the aid of these symbols, the illiterate populace could still benefit from the Gospels, much as the peoples of pre-historic times had used symbols to communicate. Illumination, because this decoration paid tribute to the Holy Word in a fashion that was thought worthy.

One of the earliest of these manuscripts which has survived to this day is *The Book of Durrow*, attributed to approximately 700 A.D. In this manuscript, one of the most popular elements of Celtic art as we know it today makes its first appearance — the interlace or woven pattern. Where the influence of the interlace came from is speculative. With the spread of Christianity from the eastern Mediterranean over central and western Europe we have a new tide of artistic influence setting in from east to west. Consequently the next few centuries of Celtic manuscript art show an evolution of style that hints of influence brought in by missionaries travelling to and from Rome, Egypt, Syria, Greece, Armenia, and perhaps Persia. In addition, the influence of the pagan Germanic peoples of northern Europe introduces a greater use of animal forms into the manuscript art.

Thus the art of the Celtic manuscript had elements of the eastern Mediterranean and the Germanic use of animals combined with the earlier use of scroll and geometric patterns. Interlace in particular was adopted as a favorite new method of ornamentation. With all of these cleverly combined, a new phase of exuberant and intricate Celtic art evolved.

Although the symbolic use of the human figure was the last to enter the Celtic artistic vocabulary, its presence in many of the later designs gave to the universe of animal and plant forms a unity and cohesion which is overwhelming in its impact. All the elements are drawn together by this dominant symbol of the human figure most effectively in the greatest Celtic manuscript we know today as *The Book of Kells*.

Many of the roots of Celtic art can be traced to pre-Christian times, yet it is after the introduction of Christianity into the culture of the Celts that their art form reaches its fullest expression. Christianity provided the vehicle for the union of all the Celtic art elements, giving expression through art a boost from the simultaneous introduction of need, motivation and purpose.

Originally, the Celtic Christian impulse swept into Ireland, bypassing England. The Irish missionaries carried their message to countries where Christianity had not yet penetrated, in particular founding monasteries in Scotland. The first of these Celtic Christian settlements was on the Island of Iona, off the Scottish west coast, in 563 A.D. It was in these monasteries that the manuscript masterpieces of incredibly intricate art were born over the next few centuries.

From around 300 A.D. onwards, the Romanised Christian Church began to penetrate Britain through the south of England. By the seventh century, clashes between the Roman and Celtic Christian philosophies were a set back to the flourishing manuscript art. From 950 to 1200 A.D. the strength of the Christian Celtic art declined rapidly.

The repeated Viking attacks which took place on the coastlines of Scotland and Ireland during this time also had a decisive effect on the manuscript work. It was no time for scribe and artist to sit with pen and brush patiently copying and embellishing the scriptures. Unfortunately, whatever recovery did follow in the eleventh and twelfth centuries, the unique and peaceful artistic structure which had prevailed earlier was now replaced by a very different one, in which warlike themes predominated.

It is important to note in passing that the decline of manuscript art paralleled an increase in the strength of the metal-worker and the stone-carver. Perhaps this is because the stones were not so easily removed and metal not so easily destroyed by the invaders.

In 1170 Ireland faced yet another invasion — that of the Anglo-Normans. Again we see the inevitable result of alien domination: the national spirit was crushed, and artistic inspiration deteriorated. In Scotland the art of stone carving continued to the early sixteenth century, but gradually the designs lost much of their original character through introduction of foreign motifs. At this time the effects of the Reformation and other political changes reduced the artistic genius and imagination of the people to a point where it did not regain its vitality as it had several times before, and the world of Celtic art entered into centuries of sleep.

Yet, in spite of it all, the old love for the curvilinear ornament and interwoven pattern has remained in the hearts of many, and occasionally makes a flickering appearance during this last century. Looking around, one can clearly see that copies of old Celtic masterpieces are becoming increasingly popular, and adaptations of old designs into pottery, leatherwork, printing and even textiles are increasing.

One of the most influential pioneers in this renaissance of Celtic art was George Bain. In his art student days during the early years of this century, his country's most natural art form was something limited to history lessons, and was not encouraged to be applied to new works as original designs were thought to be impossible. Because of the complexity of the knot and scrollwork, adaptation by copying was thought to be the only possibility, which was as valueless as it was boring for the creative young artist. So Bain proceeded on a lifetime's search to understand the essential principles of Celtic art, culminating in the publication of his book, *Celtic Art: The Methods of Construction.* In this manual he shows the logic behind the creation of the style, encouraging people to explore the unlimited potential within it.

As Bain himself says, "Duty to art is partly religion to such artists who will deliberately set aside all that they had previously valued in search of the change that must exist to allow art to live."

THE COLOURING SECTION of this book comprises twenty-six complete designs. Each design fills several pages, starting with enlargements of elements of the design and culminating in a full page reproduction which can be used as a print suitable for framing or as a gift.

Each design is initially presented two or three times to encourage a sense of freedom for you to experiment with colour combinations and techniques.

The final presentation of each design has nothing on the back but the design title and interpretation. Having experienced different colour options on the practice prints you can now apply the results to the final designs.

The choice of medium is as varied as you wish to make it. Coloured pencils and felt tip pens are the easiest to use, but other alternatives include dry brush water colour and coloured inks. The print on the cover was coloured with ink, and coloured pencils were used for the highlights and shadows.

The quotations scattered throughout the pages are for your reflection while you are colouring in the designs. They are favourites chosen by me and my friends.

Enjoy yourself

alice

*Like all young men I set out to be a genius
but mercifully laughter intervened.*

Lawrence Durrell
Clea

The Star of Unity

The five pointed star
traditionally represents perfected humanity
(with feet anchored in the earth, arms outstretched
and head in the heavens).
This design,
a single line forming two five pointed stars,
symbolises the union of Body and Spirit.

You don't tell the quality of a master by the size of his crowds.

Richard Bach
Illusions

Whatever the country, the creed or the social position of the person I approach, so long as the same fire of expectancy glows in him as it does in me, then a fundamental, final and total contact is immediately established.

Teilhard de Chardin
La Planétisation Humaine

"Outwitted"
He drew a circle that shut me out —
Heretic, rebel, a thing to flout,
But Love and I had the wit to win:
We drew a circle that took him in!

Edwin Markham

One Earth

A human figure representing the Divinity within us all
embraces the planet upon which he envisions
the harmony and unity of all mankind.

Depicted in the four corners of the border are
the faces of humanity,
the kingdoms of animal, mineral and vegetable,
an angel holding the symbol of perfected man,
and a single lined knot representing life's continuous cycle
of birth, life and death.

Decorating the throne are
the four elements, seasons and apostles
expressed in their traditional symbols of
Bull (also symbolic of Luke, Taurus, and earth),
Eagle (John, Scorpio, water),
Man (Matthew, Aquarius, air)
and Lion (Mark, Leo, fire).

Evolution
which offers a passage
to something that escapes total death
is the hand of God
drawing us to himself.

Teilhard de Chardin

Doubt is a pain
too lonely to know
that faith
is his twin brother.

Kahlil Gibran

Oh, the years of Man are the looms
of God
Let down from the place of the sun;
Wherein we are weaving always,
Till the mystic work is done!

author unknown

Attunement

*The divine group
sounds a single note.*

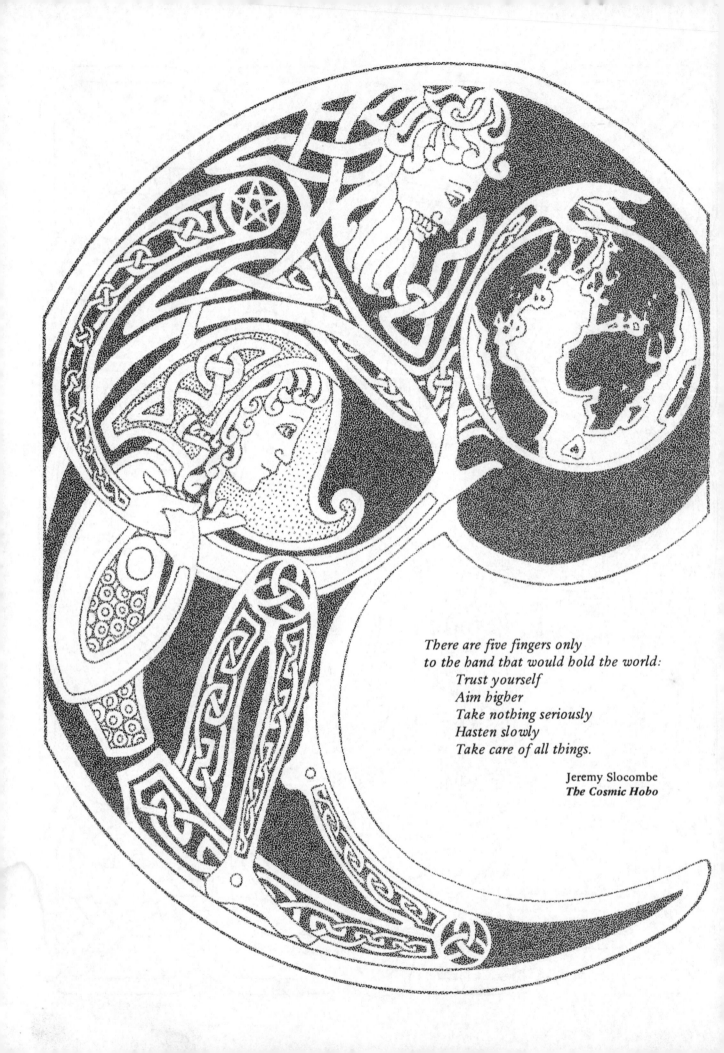

There are five fingers only
to the hand that would hold the world:
Trust yourself
Aim higher
Take nothing seriously
Hasten slowly
Take care of all things.

Jeremy Slocombe
The Cosmic Hobo

Relationship

The balanced relationship
is symbolised by the
union
of three equal parts.

The whole future of the Earth, as of religion, seems to me to depend on the awakening of our faith in the future.

Teilhard de Chardin

United Earth

Members of humanity link up
and envision a united earth
while the angels of North, South, East
and West look on.

Man is a seed
unfolding into the full potential
of his being.

*What lies behind us
and what lies before us
are tiny matters compared to
what lies within us.*

Ralph Waldo Emerson

Blind Oedipus (Mankind)
is guided by his daughters
(the visions of Love)
to his higher destiny.

The door we open
to feed the beggar
is the door
through which we are fed.

Bruce McCausland

*. . . for what is important in a man is not
so much what he achieves, but the basic
reason that inspires his activities.*

Pierre Leroy

In order to live free and happily,
you must sacrifice boredom.
It is not always an easy sacrifice.

Richard Bach
Illusions

Peace

May the angel of Peace
embrace your life
in the realising of peace on Earth.

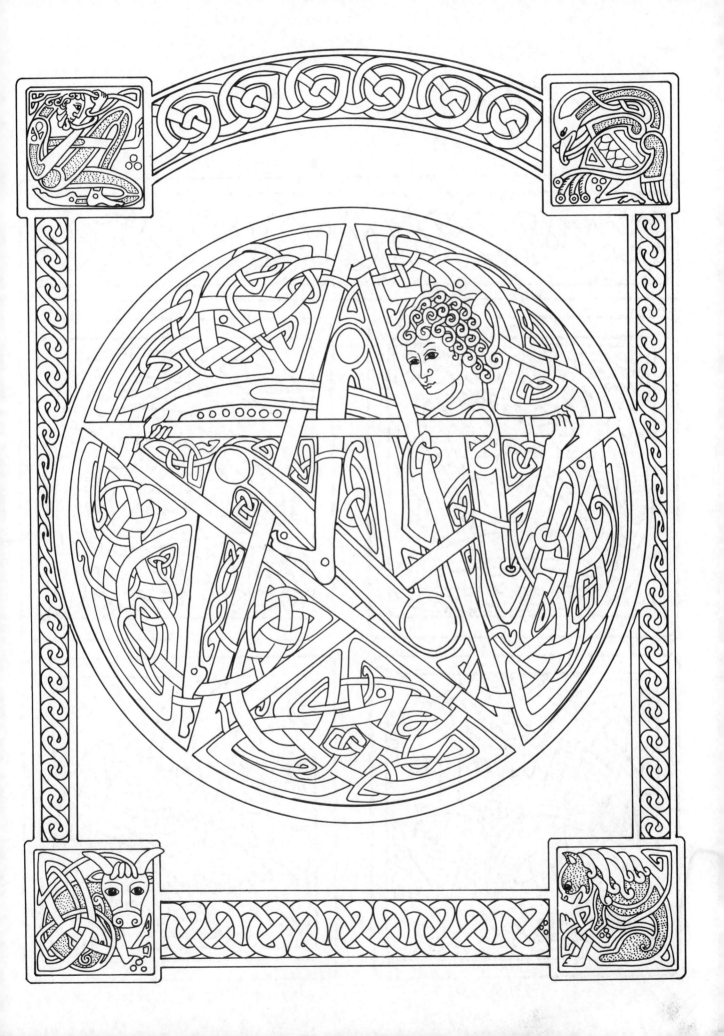

Do what you must do, and do it well:
and then pass quickly to do that
which you dare not.

Jeremy Slocombe
The Cosmic Hobo

Wisdom

"May the Wisdom within your heart
unfold into the Universe"

The five pointed star
traditionally symbolic of perfected humanity
emerges from the heart
to extend beyond the realms of our physical bodies
and into the sphere of the Universe.

Illuminating the four corners are
Man (also symbolic of Matthew, Aquarius and air),
Bull (Luke, Taurus, earth),
Lion (Mark, Leo, fire)
and Eagle (John, Scorpio, water).

It is good to have an end to journey towards; but it is the journey that matters, in the end.

Ursula Le Guin
The Left Hand of Darkness

*Argue your limitations
and, sure enough,
They're yours.*

Richard Bach
Illusions

Envisioning the 80's

*As we move into the decade of the 80's
we look towards the solutions that will synthesise
the fundamental societal aspects of
Personhood, Power and Prophecy.*

*The images within the horizontal bar of the cross
symbolise Personhood:
the art of becoming a full individual
while uniting with others in a common goal.*

*The lower half of the vertical bar
depicts a new form of Power:
a power born from the communion of many
rather than from the domination of one.*

*The top of the vertical bar
denotes Prophecy:
emphasising that by aligning ourselves
with our spiritual natures
we can prophesy the future by becoming
co-creators, and not merely victims, of it.*

*In the centre of the cross
where all unites in perfection,
is Earth
awaiting its transformation.*

*The time comes
when the true nature of man
must be drawn
from the inside out.*

Love alone can unite living beings so as to complete and fulfil them . . . for it alone joins them by what is deepest in themselves. All we need is to imagine our ability to love developing until it embraces the totality of men and of the earth.

Teilhard de Chardin

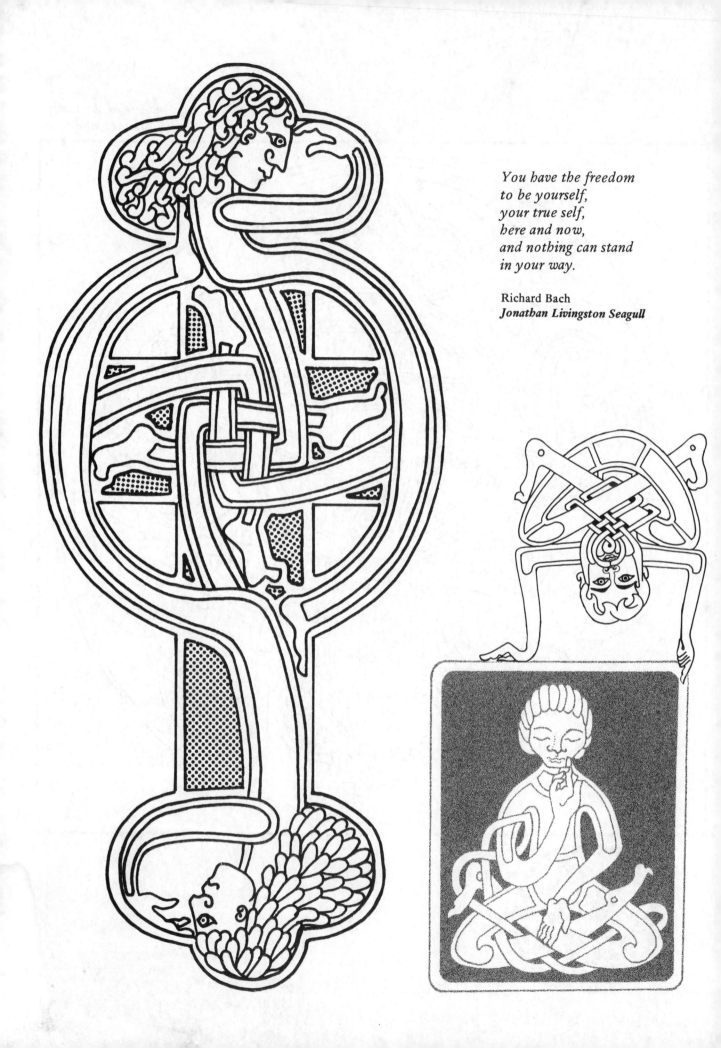

You have the freedom
to be yourself,
your true self,
here and now,
and nothing can stand
in your way.

Richard Bach
Jonathan Livingston Seagull

The Key of Life

*"Man contains within himself
the key by which his full potential
is unlocked"*

*The Labyrinth that fills the background
is a traditional ornamentation from Scotland
dating from about 500 A.D.
Known as a Key Pattern
it symbolises humanity's spiritual path.
As a "free choice maze"
in which each part is related to every other part
it offers endless choices of direction to the centre
thus enhancing the design's central theme
that individuals are co-creators of their destiny.*

Any fool can count
the seeds in an apple;
but only God can count
the apples in a seed.

Old proverb

Heavenly Father

*The strength of our Celestial Father
surrounds and supports
the nurturing Mother Earth.*

The Cross of Humanity

*"The nature of the Christ
lies within each one of us"*

*This design is an adaptation
of an Irish Celtic cross from around 1000 A.D.
The addition of the human figures
emphasises the concept that the centre of the cross
is where humanity unites to experience oneness.
This unity of mankind
results when we express the Christ within.*

As Man moves into the New Age,
he will progressively leave behind
the inflated value of the form level
and look more towards expressions of the heart.

Man cannot discover new oceans
until he has courage
to lose sight of
the shore.

Author unknown

*The three gates symbolise
the adventure of an individual's soul as it journeys
through the realms of the physical, the emotional
and the mental, in search of a greater spiritual awareness.*

The world with all its riches, life with its astounding achievements, man with the constant prodigy of his inventive powers, all are organically integrated in one single growth and one historical process, and all share the same upward progress towards an era of fulfilment.

Teilhard de Chardin

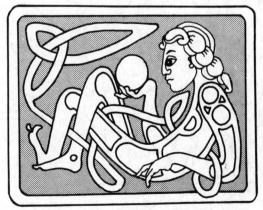

The Fates lead him who will;
him who won't, they drag.

Seneca

He who binds to himself a joy
Does the winged life destroy
But he who kisses the joy as it flies
Lives in eternity's sunrise.

William Blake

The Twelve

*Moving counter-clockwise around the globe
are twelve personalities representing
the twelve signs of the Zodiac.
The corresponding seasons appear in the four corners:
Angel—Winter
Bull—Spring
Lion—Summer
Eagle—Autumn*

*This design can also represent
the twelve apostles,
with the seasonal symbols corresponding to
the four Gospels:
Matthew—Angel
Mark—Lion
Luke—Bull
John—Eagle*

A bird does not sing be-
cause he has an answer,
He sings because he has
a song.

Joan Walsh Anglund

Harmony

*The angel of Harmony
becomes the focus through which
the many personalities of humour, spontaneity,
wit, curiosity, music, and others
begin to express themselves.*

hey gave us many presents, and we
left them the happiest people on earth,
for they had given away their very best.

Daniel Long
The Marvellous Adventures of Cabeza de Vaca

*Power motivates
the human race.
Sometimes
I think love should.*

Kelly Dunham
age 8

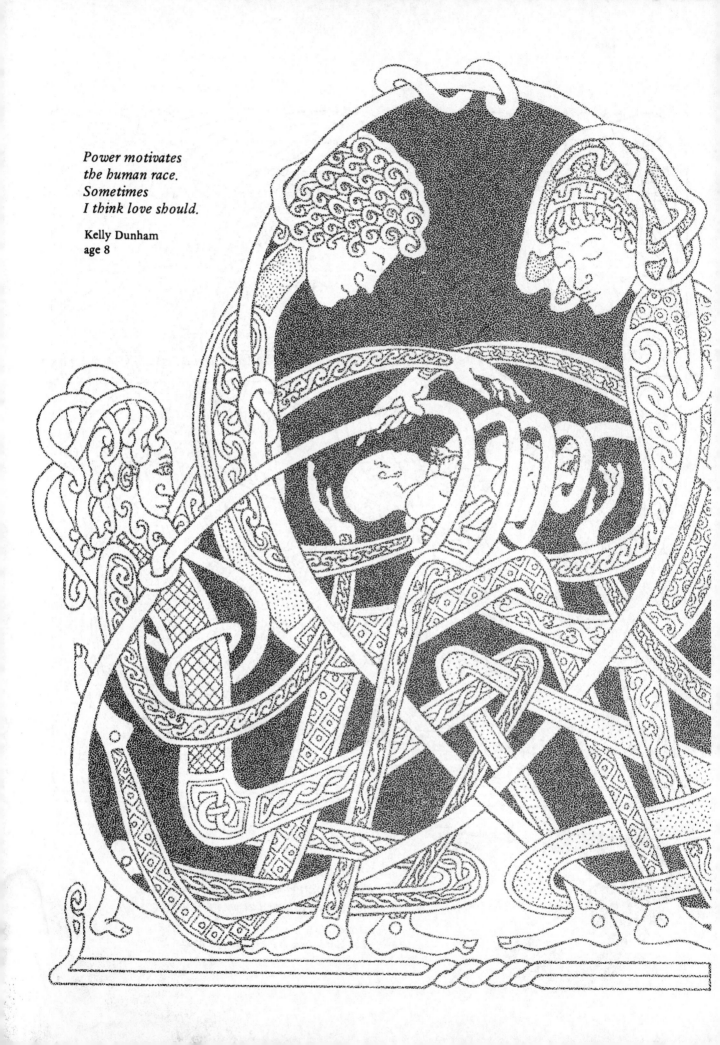

Christ Renewed

Originally conceived as a Christmas card,
this design symbolises the concept that
the spirit of the Christ child is born
within the hearts of all humanity.

The thread in the symbolic formation
of infinity and/or The Trio
binds the energy of the Christ
within the heart of every person.

The message of this design, however,
moves beyond the limits of the Christmas season,
for the nature of the Christ
lives throughout the year.

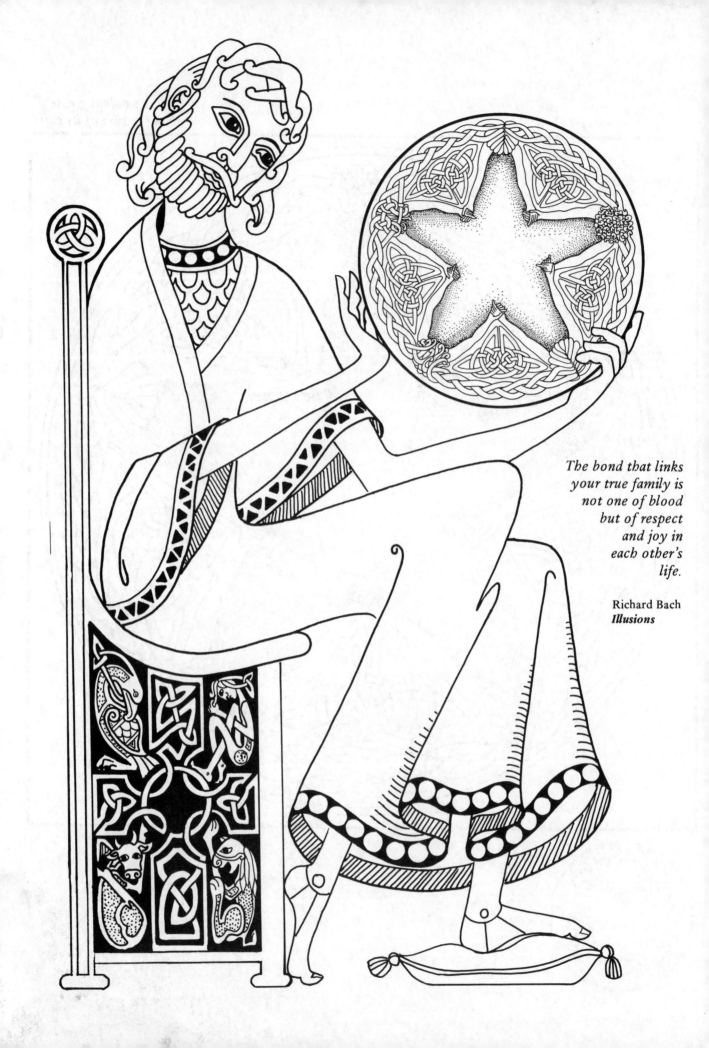

The bond that links
your true family is
not one of blood
but of respect
and joy in
each other's
life.

Richard Bach
Illusions